A Guide
For Young
Christians

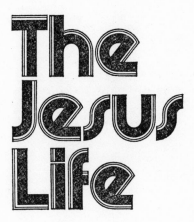

The
Jesus
Life

Alvin N.
Rogness

AUGSBURG PUBLISHING HOUSE
MINNEAPOLIS, MINNESOTA

THE JESUS LIFE

Copyright © 1973 Augsburg Publishing House

Library of Congress Catalog Card No. 72-90260

International Standard Book No. 0-8066-1307-6

MANUFACTURED IN THE UNITED STATES OF AMERICA

CONTENTS

This

Man

Jesus

He never travelled more than a hundred and fifty miles from home, and he died at the age of 33. He had no university education and he had no wealth. His few friends abandoned him in the pinch. He was executed—on a cross—as a common criminal.

Yet no one has changed the lives of so many people on the earth. And today, almost two thousand years later, Jesus still is the most honored name in the world.

Millions of churches the world around are dedicated to him. Hundreds of millions of people bear his name: Christian. In every age countless people have died rather than give up their trust in him.

How do we account for the strange power of this man?

He *is* the Son of God—there can be no other explanation. Great names have come and gone—Plato, Caesar, Augustine, Luther, Lincoln. You will find them in library stacks. But Jesus lives in the hearts of people. He simply will not rest on book shelves. He creeps into your heart and mine.

The clue is a resurrection. On Friday in Jerusalem his enemies thought they had finished him. On Sunday morning he rose from the dead. A few weeks later he returned to heaven with the promise that sometime he would come again visibly to the earth.

In those few weeks his kingdom began to take root in the world. His scattered followers took heart. Jesus was not gone after all. They had seen him, spoken with him, eaten with him, touched him. This was no dream. He had overcome death. And he had given them a vision of winning the whole world for him. "Go, and make disciples of all nations," he said. They took him seriously. Before the end of that first century they had fanned out into the entire Mediterranean world. Jesus was on the march. He has pursued kings and peasants and captured them.

He has found you and me.

If we ask the question, "What has Jesus done for me?" we are likely to come up with many different answers. All of us are different, have different needs, and respond differently.

In one overwhelming thing we have no differences. We all need God. On the cross Jesus made it possible for us to have God again. He died to forgive us all our sins, to open again the door to the Father's house, and to give us full rights to the Kingdom. We could now come to God, and God to us, with no roadblocks to bar the way. In fact, in some strange way Jesus himself is

6

God, God the son, and in coming to Jesus we come to God. Whatever else Jesus has done for us —and continues to do—by his death and resurrection he flung wide the doors to heaven for all men.

Today many people are asking the question, "What really does it mean to be a human being?" Are we any different from the animals, except that we do more clever things than they? When Jesus came to earth and became a baby, he became totally human. He was not God in disguise. During his 33 years, he went through all the things that we go through. He slept and ate, he worked and played, he enjoyed friends, he wept and laughed, he suffered pain and he died. The only difference is that he did no wrong; he was without sin. But he was human, and you and I are human. And in becoming human, he lifted "the human" up to the level that it ought to be.

We can learn a lot about ourselves by studying animals and their behavior. To determine what nuclear fallout will do to human beings, we experiment on beagle dogs. But we are not beagles; we are human beings. To know what it means to be human, we do not go to monkeys or beagles. We go to Jesus. He is the altogether complete and perfect human being.

Also, today many people are asking, "What really is the meaning of life?" Are life's longings and yearnings, pain and joy, fears and dreams— are they like disjointed pieces of a jig-saw puzzle that have no pattern or picture at all? Or, is there some great and wonderful whole—and how can we find it?

7

Jesus is the key. It is not easy to describe how. But in him all the fragments of life come together into a whole. People who have been trying to find meaning and happiness through success, through drugs and alcohol, through an endless chase after pleasures will tell you that when Jesus found them they at last knew what life was all about.

What really did they find in Jesus? They found strange peace and comfort in knowing that he forgave them all their failures and sins. They rested back in the wonderful awareness that he was as near as the air they breathed, and that he would never drop them. There were still problems and fears, but Jesus was at their side.

By finding Jesus, they found each other. Jesus loved them, and they loved Jesus. But Jesus told them that the only way really to love him was to love each other. So they turned away from themselves to be swallowed up in the needs of other people. They had never dreamed that this could be so exciting and so meaningful. All life opened up for them.

Susan had thought about herself and her wants almost entirely. She was decent to people, but she really didn't care for them. She used them. Then Jesus came into her life. She began to look away from herself—to others. She had never liked Jane. Who could care for someone who was a loner, even sullen? But now something stirred inside of Susan. Perhaps Jane was lonely; perhaps she was afraid that she didn't count with anyone. Susan set out to care for her. She went out of her way to notice her and be kind to her. And a miracle happened. Jane blossomed, learned to smile, and was drawn into a whole circle of friends. Susan remembered Jesus' words, "Whatsoever you have done to the least of these, you have done it to me."

The simple formula for great meaning in life —according to Jesus—is to turn from yourself to God and to others. You can do this because you know that you count with Jesus. You are a somebody. God created you in his image, and he died on a cross for you. What other guarantee do we need to be convinced that we count? And because we count, then all men count. I cannot now treat myself as if I don't count, and I cannot treat you as if you don't count. We are children of God, joint heirs with Christ to the riches of God's kingdom.

Wouldn't it be a pity if we bypassed Jesus and all that he can mean for us? Suppose we were to say that Jesus is O.K. for church and that there's where he belongs—and never take him with us into our fears and hopes?

Think what a vast universe he owns and manages. Think what love he must have for us to die on a cross for us. Think what full and glorious life he wants for us, and stands ready to give us.

Some of the most brilliant and successful persons in the world have found Jesus to be the key to their lives. Their knowledge and their wealth were only accidents. This did not give them meaning. It was this person, Jesus Christ, who

9

gave their life its glow. They would give up everything rather than let Jesus go.

We may be neither brilliant nor wealthy nor powerful. Who cares about that finally? We have Jesus, the Lord of the universe, as our brother and friend. And who can ask for more?

This
Lonely
World

A bus depot can be a very lonely place, with streams of strange faces going by. It might be an interesting place, but still lonely. No one bothers even to look at you.

The world can be like that—any part of the world. Even a school room can turn out to be lonely.

Each of us comes into this world alone, and each of us leaves alone. Birth and death are not for crowds. And in between birth and death, even if we have seventy years, we may keep on being alone. We need not be, but we may—if we don't do something about it.

From the start God did something about it. He had created Adam, and all the animals. Then he said, "It is not good that man should be alone," and he went on to create a companion for him and named her Eve. Ever since that time it is important for every person to have companions. It is not good to be alone—or lonely.

What can you do about it? You may be lucky and have other people do something about it. You may have a father and mother, brothers and sisters, who love you and try to be your companions. You may have friends who want to be around you. Even then, you will have to do something. You may turn them off, and finally they may give up and let you go your lonely way. You cannot have friends unless you are willing in turn to be a friend.

But being a friend is something more than making friends. If the only reason you are a friend to someone is to get his friendship in return, and if each of you sets out to "use" the other person for friendship, both of you will fail. Everything you have learned about Jesus and his way with people will tell you that this is not enough.

Jesus set out to be a friend to people, whether they in return became his friends or not. This is the nature of love. Love may turn out to be a one-way street. In fact, when he went to the cross, everyone had left Jesus to himself. But that did not stop him from being a friend. He was a friend even to the men who crucified him. He cried, "Father forgive them, for they know not what they do." And to the robber who reached out to him, he said, "Today, you will be with me in Paradise." He insisted on being a friend to everyone, even to the end, no matter whether they returned his love or not.

Jesus was never really lonely, therefore. Everyone in the world was his friend, not because they were friendly or loved him, but because he insisted on being *their* friend. He died for us all.

12

Once Jesus told a story of a man who walked from Jerusalem to Jericho and was mugged by some robbers. He told the story because a lawyer had asked him, "Who is my neighbor (friend)?" Jesus went on to tell of two men who walked by and didn't help the poor man. But a man from Samaria came by, picked him up from the ditch, bandaged his wounds, took him to a hospital, paid a deposit for his care, and promised to pay the whole bill. Then Jesus said to the lawyer, "Which of these men was a neighbor (friend) to the poor man?"

The point of the story is that this stranger from Samaria became a friend to the man. He did not ask, "Is this man in the ditch my friend?", but "Can I be a friend to him?" Perhaps he never saw him again, but he was his friend. And can you say that this man from Samaria was a lonely man? Perhaps he was never lonely—not because he had many friends, but because he was a friend to many.

If I ask you, "How many friends do you have?" you may begin to count the number of people who like you. But perhaps that is the wrong question. Perhaps I should ask, "To how many people are you a friend?" You may have many people who like you, or you may have few. And if you are always counting them, you may always be afraid of being lonely. But if you are forever looking for people to help, people to whom you might *give* friendship, will you ever be lonely?

Suppose in the fall a new girl comes to your school. Let us say that she is different, perhaps

13

an American Indian. She is quite alone. She dresses differently, and she is shy. As time goes on she grows more withdrawn. Do you ask, "What can she do for me?" or do you say, "What can I do for her?" If you set out to be her friend, introduce her to your friends, find ways to help her, perhaps invite her to join your club, have her in your home—do you think you will be lonely? By helping another not to be lonely, you yourself will find loneliness disappearing.

And don't forget what Jesus said about helping someone like that. He said, "I was a stranger, and you took me in." It is as if in helping this Indian girl you were in fact entertaining the Lord himself.

For many people this is a lonely world. And the more populated it becomes, the more lonely it threatens to be. Because, after all, it can be like a huge bus depot, with billions of people going their own way and not caring for anyone.

People work in offices, each at his desk and each hardly bothering to know the names of people at other desks. Or even in school, you hurry from one room to another, jostling each other in the halls, but never really bothering to help anyone. Or on a freeway, car after car racing along, each driver looking stark ahead, careful only not to touch any other car. Or even at home, you race in at meals only to race out again, or have a solitary session in front of the TV before mumbling a good-night and going to bed. The world can be lonely—if we do nothing to change it.

A good place to start is to remember that we

14

are never alone if we let God in. He has promised never to leave us. We can leave him, but he does not leave us. We do not see him, but he is as near as the air we breathe.

Whether you recognize it or not, the Lord came to you when you were baptized. And ever since he has been near, even when you turned away from him. You may have missed him, simply because you have forgotten about him. But he is there. If you let him do what he wants to do for you, you will never be quite lonely again.

You can talk to him in prayer. He will talk to you through his Word. You may do this alone, in a kind of private party. "He walks with me and he talks to me, and he tells me I am his own." And you may talk with him in the company of others who also talk to him—on Sunday morning in a church service.

If you really want Jesus around, you will quickly discover that you are surrounded by a tremendous crowd of people—because Jesus brings with him all those who are his—and he tells you to be their friend. Whatever you do for them, he tells you, you really are doing it for him. From that moment on, how can you ever be alone—or lonely? The whole world becomes your family.

Travel the whole world over, and you meet your brothers in every land, whether you can speak their language or not. There is a universal language, the language of love and kindness, that everyone understands. For you the world is lonely no longer!

This
Good
Earth

I get depressed. I read about fish dying in the lakes, the rivers filled with garbage, the cities overcast with smoke and gas, and even the oceans becoming too polluted to sustain life. I read on about crime in the streets, festering ghettos, wars and rumors of wars. Unless I shake myself a little, I'm about ready to give up on this world.

But I'm not ready to give up. It is a good earth. God made it good, and the carelessness of man cannot destroy it.

Whenever my mood gets too heavy, I turn to the great chapters in Genesis. Step by step, God made all things, and at the end of each step we read, "and God saw that it was good," and when he was finished, "And God saw every thing that he had made, and behold it was very good." I would rather take my cue from Genesis than from today's newspaper.

Whether I understand Genesis as a reporter's account of what happened or think of it as a poetic description, the fact remains that God made all things, and that he made them to be good. Whether God used eons of time or six 24-hour days—this is not the most important question. However long it took him, God had to be there. He alone can create something from nothing.

In any event, I believe that the earth is basically good, because God made it good. Man can mismanage it, deplete its resources, and cause much unhappiness. But I am sure that God puts limits on man's blundering, and that he will not let us destroy it. He stands ready to help us in every effort to keep it a good place.

When you study science, has it ever occurred to you how marvelously organized everything appears to be? You can count on the orderliness of the universe, all the way from the migration of birds to the wheeling galaxies. We could never have made our flights to the moon if our scientists could not have relied on the fixed "laws" or processes of nature. I once heard a great physicist conclude a lecture with these observations, "When I think of the tremendous organization of nature, from its microcosm (the smallest things) to its macrocosm (the largest, the stars), and when I face the vast unknown and unknowable of the universe, I join with the psalmist of old and say 'the heavens declare the glory of God and the firmament showeth his handiwork.'"

When a farmer puts seed in the ground, he counts on the sun and the rain and the soil to produce the wheat. When an airliner reaches a certain speed, the pilot knows that the wings will cause the air to lift these thousands of pounds into the sky. God has put things together in such a way that if we discover his "laws" and use them, certain predictable things will happen. What a great God we have to give us such a good reliable earth!

Would it not be dreadful if God had been careless and capricious, and that one year the birds would forget to migrate and freeze to death, or that one year the ground would forget to germinate the seed and we have no crops? It is not strange that most great scientists are religious people. They stand in awe and wonder before a universe of such precision and order.

In Psalm 8 the writer expresses another wonder:

"When I consider thy heavens, the works of
    thy fingers,
the moon and the stars which thou hast or-
    dained,
what is man, that thou art mindful of him?
And the son of man, that thou visitest him?
For thou has made him a little lower than
    the angels."

The most wonderful part of the earth is man. You are more mysterious and marvelous than the stars. If you ride in an airplane, it is the passengers and not the jet that should make you think of God.

After all, man is the most amazing of all creation. A great airplane, the Boeing 747, for instance, with its nearly 400 passengers, is an astonishing thing. But who designed and produced it? *Man!* The rocket that streaks through space, sometimes at 4000 miles an hour, and finally reaches the moon—this is not as fascinating as the team of scientists that produced it and the lonely astronauts who guide it. Man is the crowning creation.

The earth is good because it is the dwelling place of man—and God created man to be the best of all. A king's palace is not great because it has a hundred rooms; it is great because the king dwells within it. The earth is not great because it has mountains and oceans, but because it houses the creatures who were created in the image of God. God has put a part of his family on this earth—you and me. That's really what makes it a good earth.

God made us at great risk. There was no risk for God in creating the winds that blow or the fish that swim. These he has in absolute control, by natural instinct and by natural law. But to man he gave the gift of freedom. They alone, of all his creatures, could choose to obey him or not to obey him. He gave them freedom, because he wanted them to be like him, to live with him and to love him because they wanted to, and not because they had to.

This created trouble for God. Man often chooses not to obey God. We go our own way, heedless of what God may want us to do. The story of man, therefore, is the long story of his turning away from God and his ways. Whenever he does this, he brings himself and the world into trouble.

Whatever troubles we have on this earth, wars and pollution and crime, are not God's doing or God's will. God made everything good, and God wants to keep it good.

But even when he turns away from God, man is still the most marvelous of God's creation. We are like princes in a royal house. We are born to be sons of the great God, our king. If we fail him, we are rebellious sons. But we are princes still. He does not demote us. He does not say, "I wanted you to be a son, a human being, but because you have disobeyed me, I will reduce you to a centipede or a cockroach." We remain human beings, with freedom, and our God goes to the great lengths of a cross to try to win us back to him and his ways.

We do not know if among the billions of other planets and stars in this universe there might be some place where human beings, with freedom, may live. Up to this point our astronomers have discovered no other planet that can sustain life. There may be none. It just may be that God has no other place in this vast universe where he has colonized a race, like us, that is destined to be like him and live with him.

It is a good earth. Just look around you. There are trees and flowers, birds and fish, sunshine and rain—and there are people, wonderful people. They are not perfect. Like you, they have many failings. But what an amazing kind of creature! They have a touch of God about them—like you. And it is God's will that we make of this earth the kind of place he wants for us, his children. And be sure of this, he is at our elbows to help us in every good effort to make of our earth the kind of place he intended it to be from the beginning.

How Religious Are You?

Maybe you don't feel religious at all.

Neither church services or reading the Bible turns you on. The sermon is dull, the hymns are slow, even the prayers are unexciting. And the Bible is just so many words, rather strange words.

Does this mean that you are not a Christian?

A Christian should feel joy, shouldn't he? But you find more joy in a swift ride on a motorcycle or flying down a hillside on skis—or simply sitting around with your friends doing nothing.

And shouldn't you be full of hope, if you are a Christian? The world does not send you into ecstasy over the future. In fact, you'd like to be an ostrich and dig your head into the sand whenever you think about what the world may be like in another fifty years or even ten years.

Certainly you should feel a surge of love for God and for other people. But you have a hard time loving someone you've never seen or touched, and you may have even a harder time loving a few people that you do see and touch.

22

And shouldn't you throb with faith, if you really are a child of God? But often you have more doubts than you have faith. All sorts of questions bother you. What is life for? Where did I come from and where am I going after I die? Maybe there is no God at all.

You end up not feeling very religious at all. And the question becomes very important: if I don't feel religious, am I a follower of Jesus? Am I a Christian?

First, let us get one thing straight. God never asked us to *feel* religious. He really never asked us to feel anything at all. He was always asking us to *do* something. The key to faith and joy and hope and love is *doing*. That's where this whole business of Christian faith starts. Jesus said, "If any man's will is to do God's will, he shall know whether the teaching is from God."

At first you may feel like a phony, a fraud, a hypocrite. You don't feel like trusting a God you've never seen, but you say, "I want to trust him," and you begin by pretending to trust him. You get stubborn about it. Sure, you don't feel like trusting him. You have no great evidence that God is around and listening to you or caring about you. But you say to yourself, "No matter what, I'm going to count on him."

Or, this matter of love. God has told you to love your neighbor, especially those who are in need. You know some people who could really use a little friendship or love. But you don't like them. You feel like avoiding them. But you swallow your feelings and set about to be helpful to them.

That's a bit phony, but God tells you to start doing something for them even when you don't feel like it.

Let's be frank: how many of us can really control our feelings? Some days we feel on top of the world—"everything's going my way." Some days we feel down, way down. Nothing seems right. If people around us are cheerful, we only feel the more depressed. Feelings are really quite fickle, like the shifting winds. That's why God never commanded us to have one kind of feeling or another.

If I am really to believe in God, trust him for everything, I can't turn in on myself and hope to find this strong faith in the ebb and flow of my sentiments. I turn to him, to his Word. What has he said? I find this in the Bible. And the Bible is full of magnificent promises. You don't have to read many pages, not even many paragraphs, before you realize that this book is full of promises that he has made for you and to you.

If a dear friend tells you that he has deposited $5,000 to your account in the bank, you don't ask yourself first, "Do I feel that he has?" You trust him, you are thankful, and you plan how you will use the money.

When God's Word tells you that he has done things for you and that he will do things, it makes sense to say. "O.K., I count on you," and then you go on living as if he will surely stand by the promises that he has made. You may still feel doubts, but you now have decided to trust him, however you feel.

24

You cannot trust religious feelings. The apostle Paul felt very religious about persecuting and even killing Christians before he himself became a follower of Jesus. Religious wars have been fought by people who on both warring sides felt very religious about doing battle. It was people who felt very religious about what they were doing who crucified Jesus.

In Dostoevski's great novel, *Crime and Punishment*, a young man, Raskalnikov, convinced himself that it was right (religious) to murder a rich and cruel old hag for her hoarded money. He spent the rest of his life finding ways to make up for the wrong that he knew was not God's will at all.

Doing God's will, or following Jesus, does not always give you a good feeling. You can get high on drugs in quite a different way from getting high on Jesus. His own early disciples certainly did not feel elated about everything they had to do as his followers. They did not feel good about having children bother him, or about having the five thousand hang around for food, or about going to Jerusalem where their safety was in danger. If it had been up to their feelings alone, they would all have left him. They did not want to go where he went.

It's wonderful when young people give up drugs and promiscuous sex and find their fulfillment in Jesus, as many have done in this generation. No doubt they have had strong feelings for him. But they discover that if they are to have Jesus, and Jesus is to have them, then it is not enough to have feelings. They must *do* something. They must follow him. They must ask, "Where does Jesus go? Where he goes, I must go." And Jesus goes to all who are in any kind of need. He gets involved in the world's anguish over injustice, war, poverty, pollution. Because Jesus is Lord of all life, all life becomes the concern of his follower, whether he feels like it or not.

Faith in Jesus is not the same as feelings for Jesus. Faith is stronger than feelings. It is stronger than knowledge. Faith often becomes a sheer act of will. A person may say, "I don't feel like believing, but I want to believe." And it may very well be that if a person were to say, "I don't know whether this Christianity is true or not, but with all my heart I want it to be true," then in God's sight he has faith. A man cried to Jesus, "I believe, help thou my unbelief." God himself is the giver of faith. Of myself I cannot believe in Jesus or come to him, but the Holy Spirit works through Word and Sacrament to give me faith. He makes it possible for me to be a believer.

To be sure, feelings are important. In fact, Jesus will give us deep and lasting feelings. He will help us to feel joy, to feel repentance, to feel hope, to feel love, to feel faith. But when the dark days come, and these feelings seem to slip away, be sure of this: Jesus has not abandoned us. He does not make feelings a condition for his being with us. He is with us, even in those gloomy and depressed days when we hardly dare to think that he cares at all.

A man came once to me and said, "I feel that

God has left me." I replied, "Perhaps that does not make any difference to God." After all, God is our Father, Jesus is our great Brother and Savior. There is nothing capricious about God the Father, Son and Holy Spirit. He has promised never to leave us or abandon us. He has given us his Word. We rest there.

God
Long Ago
and Far Away

If God does not hear you when you pray, why bother with him? If he is too busy with the galaxies and quasars to listen, of what use is he? He heard Moses, but that was long ago. He sent Jesus to the world, but that too was long ago.

In this highly scientific age, does God leave man to his own skills and inventions? Why should God feed the five thousand, as in Jesus' day, when we have transportation to distribute food the world around? Why should he heal the deaf and the leper, when modern medicine has all sorts of ways to make men well? Why trust him to care for our daily needs when we have unemployment insurance, social security, and medicare? Maybe God is glad to be let off. Perhaps he says, "Go ahead, take care of yourselves—you're clever enough!"

Of course we still want someone to help us. But today vast numbers forget God and turn to the government. The government should provide jobs, control prices, feed our neighbors, and prevent crime. Why have God involved?

Is he not so busy managing this vast universe that it would be unreasonable to expect that he would take time to bother with three or four billion people on this tiny planet?

But most of us have been taught to pray to him, as if he *does* bother. In fact, we have been told that God finds each of us more important than any planet. The planet is only our home, and we who are in this home are his family. The mountains, the oceans, the fields of grain, the air we breathe —all this is maintained for us, his children. If he discovered that the Rocky Mountains stood in the way of his love for us, he would destroy the mountains. This is what we have been taught from the time we were little children. He loves us just that much.

Nor is he far away and long ago. He is here and now, just as surely as he was with Moses and Peter. The fact that we do not see him makes no difference.

Long ago, for 33 years, the world did see him. God came in his son, Jesus Christ, and since then we need not wonder what God is like. We know. God is not some cruel dictator in the sky. He is not some great machinist who keeps the suns wheeling in their orbits. He is not some selfish monarch who insists that we honor him. Jesus said that he is a great and good Father, and we are his children. Moreover, Jesus said, "He who has seen me has seen the Father, I and my Father are one." We see God in the face of Jesus.

We know hardly anything of Jesus' life until he was 30 years old. For three short years he wandered about Galilee and Judea, teaching and healing. Then one Friday in Jerusalem they put him to death for "disturbing the peace." That should have been the end of the story. But the story grew wings and circled the earth.

Jesus arose from the dead, gathered a few followers, charged them to tell the world that God had indeed come to earth, and that in his death and resurrection he had provided forgiveness of sins for the whole world. Through him all people could be brought back to God to live with him here and hereafter forever. The story spread like a tide over the entire earth. It is the story that brings God within reach for you and me.

It is a simple story, simple enough for a child to understand: "Jesus loves me, this I know, for the Bible tells me so." But it is a profound story, engaging the finest minds of the centuries.

Followers of Jesus have been gathered by the Spirit into "the one, holy, Christian, and apostolic church," his body on earth. Hundreds of millions have put their trust in him, and he has never failed anyone.

Today we have a resurgence of faith in Jesus, often among high school and college people. They give up drugs and indolent ways. They turn to Jesus. They may be called "the Jesus people," or "Jesus freaks," instead of Christians. They may have little to do with the established church for the moment. But they are children of God who have come home to God through Jesus as Lord and Savior. They have found God here and now.

And a great many find their way back to their congregations and churches and bring with them this fresh faith.

All of us are strange creatures. We alone of all the creatures God has made have this longing for eternity, for something which the world can't give. We really want God, deep down. And why shouldn't we? God put us together to want him. As far as we know, dogs and robins and monkeys don't think about God. They find what they need in this world. Not man! Even if he becomes powerful and rich, there is a deep yearning somewhere within him for something more. He wants God.

Especially is this true if he has had a glimpse of God in Jesus Christ. For then God is unspeakably beautiful and good.

Of course there are still questions that we cannot answer. Where did God come from? There is no point trying to find an answer to that. If there is a God, why does he allow wars and injustice and death? To this we find no ready answer either. Only this, that the Bible makes very clear that God did not want, nor does he want, wars and tragedy and pain. He created all things good.

When things do not go well for you, be sure of this that God is on the side of having things go better. He wants only that which is good for his children. What *you think* to be good may not always be what *he knows* to be good for you. But whatever is good for you, that is what God too wants for you.

31

Remember too that God has unlimited power. All things are possible for him. And you have every right to call upon him and to expect great things from him. The future may look puzzling, and sometimes you may give up what courage you have. But don't count God out. He may be working out things for you that are much greater than you ever dreamed could be possible.

Wouldn't it be nice if God would show his face, just once, to each of us. Why can't he give us that assurance that he is around? Some people do get some striking guarantee that God is at work. The apostle Paul did. On the road to Damascus a dazzling light struck him blind and he heard a voice, the voice of Jesus. Other people will tell you of a meteor-like moment, even a vision, when they were sure that God was there. But most of us, most of the time, will be left to believe God's holy Word and to rest back in faith that he is there. We may not see him clearly at work, but by faith we are sure that he is.

We see him most clearly on the cross. There he died for us. Can anyone do more?

When we keep our eyes on the cross and remember that great work of God for us, then we can see the traces of God's goodness in all sorts of things. He gives and sustains life for us. He gives us folks and friends. We have eyes to see color and ears to hear music. And if we let him, he guides our ways so that we find unsuspected blessings every day.

God is not long ago and far away. God is as near as our thoughts of him.

I

Was Never

Asked

It doesn't seem quite fair.

I was never asked about being born, whether I would like to *be* at all. I wasn't asked if these were the parents I would like to have. I wasn't consulted about the kind of church I might like. Nor was I asked if I would like to live in this part of the country. Nobody found out whether I would like to start school when I did. In all sorts of ways I was left out. Why wasn't I asked?

Worse still, I am told that God created me to be his child—without consulting me at all. He made me to be like him, in his image, I am told. I am given the gift of choice, the right and duty to make decisions. And I am held responsible for these decisions. In fact, God told me to have management of this world, whether I like to or not. If things go wrong, God holds me—and all people like me—accountable for the mess.

Why couldn't God have made me different? Like the birds or the fish, for instance, who have to make no decisions and who do what they do by instinct only? They all seem to do, willy-nilly, what they *like* to do. I am stuck with the duty to do what I *ought* to do, and that may not be at all what I like to do.

Of course, I can turn from what I ought to do, and simply go my merry way, doing what I like to do, whether this is what I ought to do or not. Adam and Eve did this in the Garden of Eden. They ate the fruit because they wanted to eat the fruit, even when God had told them not to eat. This brought them into trouble, and ever since when men have disobeyed God, they have been in trouble.

God was angry with Adam and Eve. They were driven out of the Garden. But there is something about God stronger than his anger. His love! He can forget his anger. He can never forget his love. It was his love that sent his only begotten son, Jesus Christ, to the world to recover mankind for his kingdom.

If, in disobedience, we drift away from God, God does not give us up. He keeps after us, like a great hound in pursuit. He does not want to let us go. After all, he loves us far more than even a mother or father may love.

This is strange of God. He has this vast universe on his hands. And there are some three billions of people on this tiny planet. Why should he bother that much with you and with me? But he does. This does not make sense, but it is so. He has us as his sons and daughters, and he does not want us in some far country, away from home.

In one sense it might be nice if you could bargain with God. Suppose you say to him, "God, I appreciate the great honor of being your son and living in the palace with you. I appreciate your having confidence in me, and your putting me in charge of the affairs of this world. But, God, please let me off. You're not counting on birds or rabbits to manage anything. Why can't I be like them, and just enjoy life?"

Fortunately or unfortunately, you can't bargain. You are not asked whether you would like to be a child of God or not. You are his child, by creation and again by redemption. Edward, a young king of Great Britain, abdicated his throne for the love of a woman who as a divorcee and commoner could not be his queen, and lived out his life away from the high station to which he was born, and in exile from his country. He was in exile, because the only way he could live within the country was to be what he was born to be, the king.

You and I can live in exile from God's kingdom too. But we will be sons and daughters in exile. We are born to be his children, princes and princesses, and nothing can change that. We may be "lost" or "dead" sons and daughters, separated from our Father and from the riches of his kingdom, but to the end—even in hell—we will be his children, lost to the glorious destiny he had planned for us.

You see, you are a child of God, not because you look like his child, act like his child, think like his child—but because he made you and claims you as his child.

Is it not wonderful that God has chosen you, created you, elected you, and designed you to be his child—without consulting you—and without conditions? Suppose he were to say that you could be his child if—and only if—you would measure up as his child. If you did not measure up, he would disown you. How dreadful that would be. We would be left in constant anxiety. Have we measured up or haven't we?

All anxiety at that point is gone. No matter how we have failed him, no matter how our ways are contrary to his, no matter how far off we have wandered, he has never let us go. We are his sons and daughters still. The moment we return to him, we have all the rights of the kingdom. He does not put us on probation. He says, "Your sins will I remember no more." As in the parable of the Prodigal Son, the Father will throw a party and say to everyone, "My son who was dead is alive, my son who was lost is found." All heaven rejoices over one sinner who repents, said Jesus.

Returning to God as a son or daughter is not all merry-making, of course. Jesus said, "Follow me," which is the clue to a life with God. And Jesus reached a cross. And who knows what sorrows, pains, and struggle a life with God may entail? How much easier to be a bird or a rabbit.

One thing is sure, however. Our success or failure in following Jesus and living the kind of life God wants us to live will not change the fact that he has made us his princes and princesses. Even if again and again we fail him, he will never turn us out. He forgives and forgives and forgives, and puts us on our feet again for another day of trying.

But as long as we stay with God and don't turn from him, the pressure will be on us. Day by day we are to become more like him, and we are to follow him where he goes. And he goes into strange places—to all sorts of people in need, into all sorts of struggle for justice and mercy in government and industry, sometimes into spots of suffering. We may fail, but on we go.

Again, he does not ask if you want to go. As a son or daughter, it is inevitable that you will go or must go—not in order to become a son or daughter, but because you are one!

You are never alone as you go. God is with you. And God has all sorts of resources that will surprise you. He works silently, but powerfully. If you are doing his will, you are within the magnetic field of his working. When you think there is no hope of accomplishing anything, suddenly things happen. When you think the try will be most unpleasant, suddenly you find reason to like it. "If God be for you, who can be against us?" said Paul. You are on the winning side. A battle may be lost now and then, but the war will be won.

If you turn against God to go your own independent way, you will discover that you are not alone either. The pressures from Satan and wickedness in the world will be glad to urge you on to your destruction.

Joshua said, "Choose this day whom you will serve; as for me and my house we will serve the

Lord." If you say "yes" to the Lord, the vast resources of his kingdom will be at your side. Whatever the struggles, there will be joy and glory in the try.

When Are You a Dropout?

He quit high school the day he was 16. Even before, he hardly had time for school. Ever since he began delivering papers at the age of eight, he was never without at least one job, sometimes three or four. At 16 he had two full-time jobs, 15 or 16 hours a day. Usually he found something extra for the weekends. His folks said they had never seen anyone as ambitious as Tom. And he saved his money.

By the time he was 21 he was modestly rich. At thirty he was worth a cool million. He kept going at this whirlwind pace. He found time to marry, but no time really to make a home, and after two years he was divorced. He never bothered to make friends, except as they might do something for him. He had no time for church or for God. When he died at 48 from a heart attack, he was hailed as a great business success. His fortune was divided among his relatives—whom he hardly knew anymore—the attorneys, and the government.

Was Tom a dropout? If he was, what did he drop out from? School? Home? Life?

How about Sam? After two years of college, he still did not know what he wanted to do. So he decided to drift around a bit. He hitched rides around the country for a year, made some good friends on the way, and visited 22 states. He wrote to his folks now and then and they sent him money when he needed some. Then he decided to see Europe, and knocked around the continent for most of another year.

Returning home, he still did not know what he wanted to do. He sat around home most of the summer, mowing the lawn and taking a job now and then. In the fall he went back to college, but for only a few months. Again he took to the road.

Now, at 35, he still does not know what to do. In the meantime he has had a hitch in the army, has had a series of short jobs, and has met a lot of people. He likes people, but rarely has any close friends. He reads a lot of books, and does well in a discussion and argument. Now and then he drifts into church, but never belongs anywhere. He has never been arrested, never in jail, never had a fight with anyone. People say of him, "Sam—Sam is a good guy, but he's never amounted to anything." Is Sam a dropout, and why?

Did both Tom and Sam drop out of life? At least life the way it *should* be lived? And if they did, what other ways are there to drop out? Are there other people, thousands and even millions, who for one reason or another are really dropouts from life? And who is to say what life is really all about?

Jesus said, "I have come that they may have life and that they may have it more abundantly." Let us agree that perhaps Jesus is the only one who has a right to say what life is about.

But, you say, Jesus died on a cross at age 33. Is that life? He dropped out of his father's carpenter shop at 30, began wandering around preaching and healing, got into trouble with the authorities, lost most of his friends, and was sentenced to death on a trumped-up charge. Is that a model for anyone who really wants a full life?

A doctor had a son whom he wanted to have follow him in medicine. He laid great plans for him. But his son got caught up with some missionaries, left his medical studies, and went overseas to win people for Jesus. After two years he caught a strange disease and died. His father grieved, but not because his son had failed to become a doctor. He was a good father, knew that his son had to find that which was important for him to do, and he grieved only because his boy's life was cut short. And he was comforted in the thought that perhaps his boy had done more good in two years than some others may have done in fifty.

You cannot measure life by its length, any more than you can determine the excellence of a painting by its size.

And you certainly cannot measure life by the amount of money a man accumulates. If that's all a person has done, he may be no better than a looter. He may be very much like a person with a

41

big bag who goes through life filling his bag. He may be dropping out from everything really important. This is not to say that a man who becomes rich is necessarily a looter. He may just be a hard worker and a wise investor. He may have done all sorts of good things along the way, and he may use the very money he has gathered to do splendid things for other people.

Jesus has a very simple formula for life. We are to find people to help. This may mean that we have a job, otherwise we may not have anything to help with. It also may mean that the job itself cannot take all our time, otherwise we will not have any time left for other people.

Most of all, it means that we will have to be on the alert to find people who need our help. Jesus was always running into people who needed him. And he always had time for them. Many were not attractive. Some were even hostile to Jesus. But if they had needs—that was enough for him. He reached out to help them.

You don't have to wait for graduation to begin this kind of life. In your school, in your neighborhood, anywhere, you can find young and older people who wait for your friendship. If you can stop brooding over your own problems and turn to do something for someone else, you'll be on the way of life.

It may not be more than a cheerie "Hi." Someone has said, "It was only a glad good morning, as she passed along the way; but it spread the morning's glory over the livelong day." It may only be stopping to help someone change a tire.

In one of the lavish seaside parks, a man's Cadillac suddenly rolled to a stop. He didn't know what was the matter with his motor. While he stood alongside his car looking for help, one after another of large, sleek cars sped by him. Then came an old, noisy jallopy with some long-haired hippies. They stopped with a friendly greeting, "What seems to be the matter?" They took a look at his motor, but were baffled; they piled him into their car and took him to the nearest garage. The man told his friends, "I was reminded of the story of the Good Samaritan. My well-dressed friends passed me by." Total strangers had become his friends, and you can be sure that he no longer judged people's characters by the length of their hair. He probably had a new idea of who were the dropouts.

Many people think the future looks dark. They worry about war, the bomb, pollution, unemployment, overpopulation—all sorts of things. If they are young, they may even wonder why they should go to school at all, or why find a job at all. They become sort of paralyzed. Of course, there are problems. There have always been great problems for the world. Read a bit of history, and you will know.

But that's no good reason for dropping out from life. Every day dawns new with all sorts of possibilities for being kind to someone, for studying hard in preparation for significant service, for doing well any sort of job.

Jesus told us to pray, "Give us this day our daily bread." This day—today—is given us. Tomorrow is not yet. We may not live more than today. Who knows? Why sit around moping or twiddling our thumbs, worrying about tomorrow, when today is throbbing with things to do?

Tomorrow is in God's hands. Be sure of this, if we don't drop out from today's interesting world, he will have a very important place for us in his tomorrows.

Where Was God?

Where was God when Jim died? His motorcycle had slipped on wet pavement and thrown him. The ambulance sped him to the hospital and he had doctors waiting. As the night wore on, the kids had formed a "prayer brigade." They prayed all night. In the morning Jim died. Where was God?

Where was God as the war kept on, year after year? Millions were praying for it to stop.

Where was God when the tornado raced through the town? Where was he when the rains did not come and the crops withered in the field? Where was he when the rains swelled the streams and rivers and whole villages were destroyed?

Doesn't God bother to hear? When people cry to him with all their hearts, does he still keep stubborn silence? Is he asleep? Is he too busy with the wheeling stars to bother with people? After all, this is but a tiny planet in the vast complex of stars and planets under his care. Perhaps it's too much to expect of God to trouble himself with the prayers of us tiny people on this tiny ball.

Or, does he have a totally different idea of what is good and what is bad? Did he think it was good for Jim to die? Does he think it is good to have a war go on? Are tornadoes and drought and floods a part of his plan for us? After all, he did say, "My thoughts are not your thoughts, neither are your ways my ways."

Who has not asked these questions, over and over?

Let us first agree that we may not find any good and clear answer. Life is not as clear as the nose on your face. There is mystery. When you ask the great questions, "Where did evil come from?" and "What is the ultimate purpose of life?" you will have to choose between several possible answers.

For us who have grown up in the Christian faith, we at least have a starting place. We begin with Jesus. We believe that he was God come to earth. If we want to know what God is like, and what he may be doing about things, we take a solid look at Jesus. We read the four Gospels and get a feel of what Jesus is like. Then we can go on to ask, "Would Jesus have wanted Jim to die?" "Would Jesus like a war to go on?"

We will answer, "No, of course not!" It is impossible for us to think of Jesus wanting either. He loved everybody. He went about doing good for everyone. He died on a cross to forgive the sins of everyone in the world. He was on the side of life, not death. He said, "I have come that you might have life and that you might have it more abundantly."

46

But does God want one thing and Jesus another? Certainly not, for we believe that Jesus is God, the Son of God, the second person of the holy Trinity. "I and my father are one," he said.

Now we get to the great truth of the Bible. The Bible tells the great story of how God created man in his own image, to live with him forever. It goes on to tell how man turned from God, followed the enemy of God, and lost his place with God. In his disobedience of God, he brought all sorts of wickedness and unhappiness upon himself. In fact, much of what happens on this earth is the result of man's own blundering and sinfulness.

Even death. Death, according to the Bible, was not in God's plan. Death came in through the back door. God did not want death at all, whether Jim's or the boys' who die on a battlefield.

But, we ask, could not God have stopped all this? Could he not have stopped man from disobeying him?

Yes, he could. But at a price that he did not want to pay. He had given freedom to man. He wanted us to love him and obey him because we *wanted* to, not because we had to. He did not want us to be puppets. He had created us to be like him, with the gift of freedom. I can choose to obey God, or I can choose to disobey him. It was only to man that he gave this gift and right. He did not give it to dogs or to the winds. Dogs do things from instinct, and the winds are controlled by laws of nature. Man is the only "wild" animal who need not be governed by instinct or by the laws of nature. Man can choose. Like God, he has the gift of freedom.

Suppose you have diabetes. If you eat too much sugar you are in trouble. Your doctor gives you a diet, and asks you to observe it. He prescribes insulin. If you follow the rules of your doctor, you will be o.k. If you do not, you are in trouble. You may even die. Your parents and the doctor, if they wanted to, could put you in a room, lock the door, and make sure that you would never eat what you should not eat, and that you would take the proper amount of insulin at the proper time every day. But, you no longer would be free. You would be a prisoner. You would have no decisions to make. They would all be made for you. Would you like that?

God did not lock us up. He does not force us to obey the rules that will give us life and happiness. He gives us the rules. But he lets us be free to obey them or to disobey them. If we disobey them, we are in deep trouble. And God is grieved. But rather than take away our freedom, he lets us go our way, even if that way ends in disaster, even if that way keeps us from him forever.

Of course, Jim did not do something wrong that deserves death. Nor are the boys who die in war criminals for obeying the call of their country. Why, then, should they die?

This is the hard question. The only answer is that somehow in this vast order of things, in spite of all the questions we cannot answer, God is still on the side of life. He did not want it this way. When Jim died, God suffered too. He grieves with us who grieve. And he weeps over any war that keeps taking lives of people.

The whole thrust of the story in the Bible is that God wants only that which is good for his people. That which is not good is not of God.

The important thing to remember is that God picks up the pieces. When things go wrong for us, he does not leave us. He did not want Jim to die. But, if we will let him, perhaps he can do some rather fine things with us as a result of Jim's death. And he does not give up on Jim. When death is done with him, and can do no more, God puts Jim on his feet again in another part of his vast empire, and will give Jim a better life than he could ever have had on earth.

But we will have to trust God. Even when we don't have all the answers, we will need to rest back into the everlasting arms of God's love. If we see God in the person of Jesus, we will know that he wants nothing but good for us.

Jim won't come back to us. We must lay his body to rest in some graveyard. A war may not stop. Tornadoes and floods may come. But we can rest assured that God has not given up. We can know that he does hear our prayers. He will open doors of joy for us, if we will let him. And he hopes that we will seek his will and try day by day to do what he wants us to do. He will forgive us when we fail him, and help us to try again.

And when this life is over, he will take us to be with him in a part of his vast kingdom that is far better than anything we could ever imagine.

Is
the Holy Spirit
Something Special?

The Bible uses terms like "the gift of the Holy Spirit," and "filled with the Holy Spirit," and "baptized with the Holy Spirit," as if this may be some sort of special experience which Christians ought to request or cultivate.

No matter what conclusion we reach in understanding this language, one thing is certain. You must not divide God. God is *one*. We speak of God the Father, God the Son, and God the Holy Spirit. But God is one! We can as rightly speak of "the gift of God" and "filled with God." In fact, it may be as wise to think in terms of the one God who reveals himself as a loving Father and as a redeeming Son and as an indwelling Spirit, without attempting to assign specific functions to the three persons of the Godhead.

Another thing to remember is that we are saved by grace through faith. God's action for our salvation is called *grace;* our receiving of this action is called *faith*. Nothing more is needed. No long inventory of works and no catalog of experiences! We trust his Word that he has created us to be his children and has died on a cross to recover us as children. This trust, whether it is accompanied by feelings of ecstasy, calm, doubt, even despair—this trust is the faith.

If you have faith, mixed as it may be with many moods, you have God. To a person whose mind and heart are tipped in faith toward God's Word, God may or may not give a number of gifts. After all, God is around and is at work within you. Who knows what wonderful things he may give you?

The chief gift will be love. All other qualities fade by comparison. Read 1 Corinthians 13. Any other gift or fruit or quality which God will give you cannot compare with this supreme gift. God is love. God's kind of love (which is the kind he wants to see in us) is not sentiment or emotion necessarily. It is not necessarily an expansive feeling toward all men. You may love someone as God loves, and not like things about him at all. But you set out to help him, to be concerned about him. The love you have for God gets transferred to your brother, and you may not like your brother. He may be quite unattractive to you, even repulsive. The Lord says that this is unimportant. What you have done for him, you have done for me, Jesus says.

If you were to wait until your feelings catch up with the Lord's command, you might wait a long time. God says in effect, "I don't care how you feel about him; go and take care of him."

The fact is that God never commands us to have one kind of feeling or another, one kind of experience or another. He simply says that if we trust him we are to do what he tells us to do. He may, or may not, give us feelings of joy or hope or affection or patience on the way. We are to trust him enough to do what he tells us to do. That's enough! He may give more, he may not.

To some people, like Paul on the Damascus road, he gives a blazing experience. Paul was blinded by a bright light, he heard a voice. But in all his epistles Paul hardly mentions his own singular experience. Why? Because Paul knew that the experience was not the same as faith. He knew that most people would have to get along without this kind of feeling, and that people without that striking experience may indeed be stronger in faith than he. Faith is not built on experience; faith is built on God's Word.

Some people have been given the experience of extraordinary healing. The doctors had given up. Everyone had given up. People kept on praying, however. And healing came. No one, not even the doctors, could explain it. But you dare not build your faith on this. Thousands of prayers for healing have not stayed the hand of death. If extraordinary healing comes, thank God, but do not be audacious enough to say that in some way your faith was strong enough to wheedle God. Let it remain a mystery.

Some people, a few, have the gift of tongues. It seems that God gives them a new kind of language to use in thanking and praising him. If they were to conclude that their faith was the stronger, and that therefore the Lord awarded them a new language, they would be misunderstanding the nature of both grace and faith.

The danger of extraordinary experiences, like healing and tongues, is that people may become so engrossed in these secondary and peripheral things that they forget the nature of faith. They may even substitute experiences for God and worship the experience. It is almost as if a lover gives his sweetheart a car, and she becomes so enraptured by the car that she forgets her lover. She did not love him more because he gave her a car; in the end she maybe loved him less, and almost forgot about him because of the car.

In one sense faith is at its best, its most glorious form, when it is not braced or supported by anything at all. When Job in the Old Testament story had lost everything that might assure him that God cared for him—he had lost his property, his family, his health—it was then that he said, "If he kill me, yet will I trust him" His faith was now superb. It rested on no evidence of God's love at all; it produced no ecstasy or peace at all.

You say, "Well, read the story of Job to its end. God did show him that he loved him after all." Yes, of course. No believer will be without evidence of God's love. This evidence will come in strange ways. The ultimate evidence will always be the stark fact that some two thousand years ago Jesus Christ died on a cross for our sins. Nothing can compare with that evidence.

But you and I will see God's love in all sorts of places and ways, once we have seen it at the foot of the cross.

We will know his love in the friends we have, in the health he gives, in the touch of our beloved's hand, in the wind that blows and the sun that shines. We will find God's love lurking behind everything good that comes to us. All this is the work of the Holy Spirit who gives faith and who opens our eyes and ears to the blessings of God.

Let us be sure of this: God is around and is anxious to do for us much more than we dare to think or ask—or receive. Once he has given us himself by grace through faith, he will—if we let him—add all sorts of extra dividends or blessings.

But it is very important to keep them as dividends, extras, and not have them be the fruits or outcome of faith. You dare not say, "My brother was not killed in Vietnam because our family had such great faith," when other boys were not spared in Vietnam. Nor dare you say, "I was given the gift of tongues, because I have a strong faith," when most of the Christian family may never receive the gift, and many of them perhaps with a stronger faith than you.

The great work of the Holy Spirit is to bring us to Christ and keep us for Christ, and help us to follow him and become daily more like him. This he does as he works quietly through Word and Sacrament. If we think of God as three persons, God the Father, God the Son, and God the Holy Spirit, we may think of the Holy Spirit as God present with us, brooding over us, judging us, calling us, and nudging us farther and farther into the wonders of the Kingdom of God.

Thank
God
for What?

On Thanksgiving Day everyone in the room was listing the things for which he was thankful. Grandma, a shrunken little lady of 80, said with a twinkle in her eyes, "I thank God that the two teeth I have left meet."

Some people have a hard time being thankful. They tend to look at all the bad things in life. They become depressed. Everyone else seems to be better off than they. Even when things are going well they say, "It can't last."

Life is made up of the good and the bad, the pleasant and the unpleasant. If you keep your eyes on the good and the pleasant, you can be thankful. But if you get in the habit of looking on the dark side, you simply cannot muster any real gratitude—and you will be continually unhappy.

If you want to stay ungrateful, perhaps you should not read the rest of this chapter, because I want to review the list that makes me thankful. After all, there are people who like to complain, and if they have nothing to complain about they may be unhappy over that. I don't think you are like that—so read on.

I'm thankful for life itself. Even when the going is rough, I still want life. Perhaps my classes have been dull. I can't get a job. My best friend has moved out of town. I don't get any inspiration from church. I wake up each morning wondering what to do. Sometimes I get real low, but I haven't yet said—at least seriously—"I wish I was dead."

A friend of mine, after a very serious heart attack, recovered to live many years in good health. I remember him lying on a couch, looking around at his friends, and saying, "You'll never know how good it is just to be alive." Another friend, paralyzed with arthritis, and fastened to his bed day after day, told me how good God was to him just to let him live.

For most of us, if we have our health and a few friends, life is good. We would not want to give it up. Only a very few people get to the point where they become so discouraged that they end their lives in suicide.

Then, *I am thankful that I have eyes to see and ears to hear.* Sometimes I get too busy to look at the rich green of a springtime, the sparkling snow of winter, the riot of color in the autumn trees, and the blazing glory of a sunset. But that is my fault. It is all there for my eyes to see. I forget too to listen—to the crickets, the birds, the sighing of the wind, the laughter of people. All of this is God's music. There are people who no longer see, and people who no longer hear.

56

Strangely enough, when I meet these people they have usually discovered things to be thankful for, and rarely are they complainers. Helen Keller, who could neither see nor hear, became one of the sweetest people of our time.

I am glad I have a country. The newspapers and TV are often full of the things that are wrong with our country, and of course there are many things not right. But, ask yourself, where else would you like to live? People who have moved away, often return to say, "My country is best, after all." God has given each of us a land to love, to cherish, and to serve. Its shortcomings and problems are only reasons to love and serve it the more. The great hymn, "America, the Beautiful," may not always describe what the country is like, but it does spell out the hopes and dreams we have for it, and I want to have a part in making those visions come true.

I am happy to have a home. It is not always what it ought to be, and I am partly responsible for its failures, but it is my home. I have had grandparents and parents who loved me. They were not perfect. They failed me sometimes, and they knew it; but I failed them too. Each of us has his place in making it the kind of home it should be. Where homes have collapsed, usually God has provided some new friends who have given the strength that the home should have given.

I am thankful to be living in the last part of the twentieth century. I have lived most of the first two-thirds of this century. In my childhood, we had no electricity in our home, no running water, no telephone, no automobile, no radio, and no television. I would not like to go back to those days of inconvenience. I loved it then, but I am glad science has made such advances. I like television, and I like running water.

Since the days of my childhood we have had two world wars and a few smaller ones. The world has doubled in population. Lakes and rivers are threatened with pollution. And there is the bomb. Despite all this, I am thankful that so many new things have been discovered. The very inventions that now are a danger to us are at the same time a new hope. We have resources of power that, properly used, can take away from the entire world the century old burdens of drudgery, hunger, and war.

At times you may think that this is the worst time in the world's history. You may even think that the world cannot survive, and that you will die in some vast explosion. Try to look at the other side. With all these new resources, it could be that you and your children will live in a world much better than any other period of the world's history. Be thankful that you were born to this time, and not a hundred years ago or two hundred years ago.

The most important reason of all to be thankful is that we are God's children. You cannot change that, even if the world blows up. And if it does blow up, God puts us on our feet again in another part of his vast empire. He raised Jesus from the dead, and he will raise us from the dead too.

Let us not forget what we have probably heard from the time we were little children. The old, old story of Jesus and his love has been a part of our lives. We may not have thought the story too important, but it is the most important story ever told. It tells us that God so loves us that he gave his only Son, Jesus Christ, to die for us on a cross and to rise again on the third day. He died and rose in order that we might have our sins forgiven and that we might live with him here and in heaven forever. There is no story like it in all the world.

Ask yourself, why did God do this? The only answer is, he loves us with an everlasting love. You can't stop him from loving you. You may turn from him, and refuse to receive his love. But he is waiting around every corner to hold you, to guide you, to comfort you and to give you all sorts of things to make life a full life for you. Don't ever sell God short. He is anxious to give us much more than we can ever imagine.

Two old people stood watching their little home burn to the ground. Everything they owned was in that home. It was a very sad moment. Suddenly, Mary took her husband's hand and said, "John, we still have each other."

No matter what happens, we still have God. If every friend turns you down, you have One who never turns away. If every hope seems to be shattered, God is still there. He will never leave you. And, remember this, he loves you more than any mother or father or friend ever could. Remember also, that he has more "tricks up his sleeve," more power and resources to help you than you could ever dream of.

We can be thankful for a hundred different things—if we give ourselves a chance to think of them. Most of all, we have God. He will bless us in ways that are so lavish that we hardly dare to think of them or ask for them.

Those
Hundred-and-One
Rules

Life is full of rules. I drive down the street and suddenly I am told to STOP. In a moment I am told to GO. I read the Ten Commandments: Thou shalt not, thou shalt not. I see signs everywhere: No Trespassing, Keep Off the Grass, Private—Keep Out.

Parents have rules, the government has laws, and God has commandments. I am hedged in on every side. If I obey the rules, I am a good boy; if I break them, I am very likely in trouble. Some of the rules make sense; others I think are silly.

I break rules. I guess everybody does, sometimes. Occasionally I feel good, or a bit brave and heroic, when I break a rule. Most of the time I feel just plain guilty. Why have rules at all? Wouldn't life be more simple and happier without them?

My dentist gives me rules: Brush your teeth twice a day. Clean between the teeth every day with dental floss. Massage the gums. When I come to have a few cavities filled, he says gently,

"You didn't observe the rules, did you?" Now, there's nothing mean about my dentist. He does not love to tyrannize me. He gives me rules. He ought to be glad that I disobey them. If everyone obeyed them, he would have very little business.

The policemen ought to be glad that people break the rules, shouldn't they? After all, what would they have to do without lawbreakers around? Yet, the fact is that most policemen would be delighted if all they had to do was to remind us of what the rules are, and would never have to levy a fine or make an arrest.

Let us ask ourselves, how do rules come to be and who makes them? And why?

A mother and father who love their children and who have many years of experience behind them want very much to protect their children from harm. So, they have some rules for their children. Sometimes they seem overprotective and have too many rules, but this is out of love and not from wanting to crush their children. Few parents love to make rules or demands simply to feel important.

If I were the wisest man on earth and if I were the most unselfish man on earth, then I could get along without laws and rules. But I must admit that I am *not* always either wise or good. I do what I *want* to do, not what I *ought* to do. And what I want to do is not always good either for me or for anyone else.

In the Bible we are told of the disobedience of Adam and Eve, and then, chapter after chapter, we read about the wickedness of man. God had to give them commandments, rules to warn them against that which would harm them. God is neither cruel nor vindictive. He does not love to give laws and to punish. He loves us all, more than any human being can love. He wants only the best for us. His laws are given to keep us from hurting ourselves and each other.

A government is not God, of course. But the laws of the land are the result of the accumulated wisdom of the people down through the years. We have found ways to help one another from harming each other, and we have found ways to have each person do his part in having a better country. So we have laws. The government says that you must go to school until you are 16. You say, what business is that of the government? Only this, that if great numbers of young people dropped out of school or never went to school at all, together as a people we would not have the skills and knowledge to make life good for all of us.

The law says you cannot drive a car until you are 16 and then only if you have passed a driver's tests. Perhaps you were able to drive at 12, and perhaps you are a careful and skilled driver. But would you want to give up the law? Would you want anyone to drive at any age and without any training? Would you like a government that did not bother with the safety of its people?

Laws are to protect your rights against the carelessness or the wickedness of other people— and to protect their rights over against your carelessness or wickedness. This limits the freedom of all. We cannot do what we want to do, if this wrongs others. Even in as small a matter as noise there are rules. A group of young people may in their thoughtless enthusiasm make too much noise in some neighborhood, at night when older people may want to sleep. Now, there is nothing wrong with laughter and good fun. But a policeman may come and say, "Sorry, you must move on; you are disturbing the peace and that's against the law!" Nor does that mean that either the policeman or the people in the neighborhood are against young people or against fun. You have every right to fun if it does not violate someone else's right to have necessary peace and rest.

And how about simply keeping quiet and orderly in a school room or in a class? If in your freedom you carry on in such a way that others cannot study and learn, you not only break a rule, but you are robbing others of their right to use time and opportunity for something they want. And not only for something they want, but for something the country wants from them and from you. Vast sums of money are invested by other people to equip you with the knowledge that will be good for the country itself. The school has every right to punish you and even expel you.

Rules are made by man, and most of them are good. Sometimes, however, the laws of man are different from the laws of God, and then we must obey God rather than man. This does not happen often, but it does happen.

If a government were to pass a law that you could not go to church and you could not read the

Bible, you would have to disobey the laws of the land. This happened in the early life of the church, and it has happened in this century too. Throughout history we have had many, many people die a martyr's death, or suffered long imprisonment, because they defied the laws of their government to obey God.

You are not likely to face this. You live under a government that encourages the worship of God. But there are similar situations. Supposing you run around with a crowd that adopts a style of life you know to be contrary to Christ's ways. If you go the way of Christ, you may be dropped by the crowd. Then you suffer a kind of rejection or martyrdom. And it hurts.

A friend of mine was a partner in a very profitable business. He disagreed with some of the policies or rules of the business. He regarded them as unethical, wrong, contrary to the commands of God. Rather than go along, he sold his share of the business, at a great financial loss to himself. He chose to obey God rather than man.

God has given us a basic set of rules in the Ten Commandments. Jesus expanded and intensified them. In fact, he summarized all the commandments into one great one, "You shall love the Lord your God with all your heart and with all your soul and with all your mind and with all your strength . . . and you shall love your neighbor as yourself."

Every rule of God given in the Bible must be understood as helping us to love God, to love our fellowmen, and to love ourselves. You see, we do not even have a right to hurt ourselves, because God owns us. It is never right to say, "What I do does not hurt anyone, only me, and I have a right to do with myself whatever I want to do."

Most rules are good, whether they are made by parents, by the school, by governments, by society in general. And all the rules of God are good.

What Is There
to Like
About the Church?

I don't like everything, that's for sure. But I like some things, in fact many things. That's why I keep going. Oh, I've had stretches when I forgot to go, weeks on end. But even then, I didn't give up on the church. I'd think of it as a kind of home, a second home.

And I'd come back. Something drew me. It wasn't just the hymns or the sermons or the building. It wasn't just the people, although many of them were my truest friends. It was all sorts of things put together, I guess. And behind everything, God. Because even when I was away from the church, I was never really away from God.

I know God is not trapped in a church alone. He is everywhere. But I also know that there is no other building, no other place, especially set aside for God. I roam the streets, visit my friends' homes, sit at school, drive around, work at a job. I know that God is never far away. But none of these places has God's label. Only the church has his name on the door.

Perhaps God means more to me than I know. From the time I was a baby, I have heard his name and word and very early I learned to fold my hands and pray to him. There have been times that he has seemed very near. Many of these times were in the church. Deep down I know that God matters. When I come to die, he will mean more than all the world. And not only when I am to die. Because if he means that much at death, he probably means just as much in life too.

Long before I could think, my parents took me to the church to be baptized. I cannot understand baptism. But a whole congregation surrounded me at that moment; and now when I am a part of that congregation and a baby is baptized, I have a strange and wonderful feeling. God is adopting this child, making him a member of his everlasting family, and writing his name in his heavenly books. Long ago, the church did that for me— and I belong.

My confirmation day was something special too, although I think it has meant more to me afterward than on that day. I can't forget that I made some promises to God. I don't know how serious I was at that moment. Maybe I was a bit too self-conscious. But, when I think of it, it was a very important day. I meant it when I made my confession.

I remember when Grandmother died and we had her funeral in church. She was a wonderful person and I know she loved me. Others cried and I did too. It was sad, but it was nice too. The pastor told us how God had now put her on her feet again in heaven, where she would be waiting for us. He talked of a "great cloud of witnesses," a sort of bleacher-crowd gathered around God, cheering us on, even though we could not see them anymore. I left the church feeling almost glad that my grandmother could move on to such a wonderful place.

When my sister was married, everything was happy, except that she and mother cried a bit. But they cried out of joy, I knew. I liked her husband and was glad that he would now be my brother. I'll never forget how nice the church looked.

When I stop to think of it, the church is the place where both the sad and the glad are mixed together. And it's for real. It's not like the movie theater where everything is simply pretending. No doubt the reason the church is real is that God really is there. Jesus said, "Where two or three are gathered in my name, there I am in the midst of them." He must be there.

Once I dropped in on a church service where I did not know a single person. They were all strangers. Even here, though, I felt that I belonged. I sang the hymns with them. I heard the familiar words from the Bible. I joined them in prayer. I heard a sermon about Jesus and his love. It didn't seem to matter that I was a stranger. In fact, I didn't feel like a stranger. I felt that I belonged to them, and they belonged to me. Perhaps that's what I always meant when I confessed, "I believe in one holy, Christian, and apostolic church."

I may be a bit funny, but I think I like singing hymns best, even better than listening to a sermon. And I like old hymns, the ones I learned when I was little. Oh, I like some of the new ones too, especially those we sing with a guitar. But I guess it's the old ones that catch me where I feel it. Maybe I listened to them when I was still a baby. Some psychologists say that what you learn before you are five years old is the most important of all. I'm glad my parents took me to church when I was still a squirming kid.

It's possible to like going to church even when nothing in the service that day seems to do anything for you. This I learned one time in confirmation when the pastor asked us why we went to church. After a long discussion we came to the conclusion that the reason we went to church was that we had an appointment to thank and praise God. If the hymns were strange and if the pastor's sermon that day was dull, so what? We had come to meet and thank God. It was like making a date to pray to him and to thank him. I felt lousy, so what? Did that matter? I could thank him just as well if I felt down as if I felt high.

After all, I had a lot of things to thank him for. Most of all, I had to keep on thanking him, day after day and year after year, for letting me be his own. I know I do not deserve it. I know that Jesus died on a cross to let me come back to God, my sins all forgiven. I go to church to hear this old, old story again and again, and to thank him.

I grew up in a city church, but I always liked to visit my grandparents' church. It was a white wooden church with a steeple, out in the country. And it had a bell that tolled just before the service began and when it was over. Alongside of the church was a cemetery. My grandfather took me through it one day, after church. He pointed out the markers for my great-grandparents, some uncles and aunts, many cousins. He said, "Here they sleep, but they have gone on to be with the Lord, and one day they will all rise again." I can't quite understand how this can be, but I had a feeling that I belonged to a great company on earth and in heaven.

I hope I never drift away from church. I've seen people do just that. They get too busy, or they get caught up with all sorts of things for weekends and forget about church. God does not let them go, I know; he'll stick by them. But they miss praying to him and praising him. They forget to thank him. And that's bad, really bad. Because God gives us everything, the least we can do is to set aside an hour now and then to thank him.

Why

Read

the Bible?

Year after year, the Bible is the world's bestseller. It is translated into more languages than any other book. It probably has shaped the world's thinking more than any other book. And yet, more Bibles are lying around unread than almost any other book.

Are you reading the Bible?

If you are not, I can think of several reasons why you leave it untouched. First, you think it's too hard to understand. But certainly there are parts of it that you can easily understand: the many fine parables that Jesus told, for instance. Or, you think it's an old book, and you had better pick up some more up-to-date volume. But remember an old book that is good has more to say than some new book that will be forgotten next year. Or, you think some pastor or scholar can read it, and you in turn read or hear what the pastor says about it.

The fact is that the Bible is a special book, God's Word to us, and it is his will that everyone read the Bible. We are not to take its truths only second-hand, like letting a doctor read a medical book and then listening to the doctor.

The very most important reason for you to read the Bible is that God wants to reach you, and he uses the Bible to get inside of your heart. Only the Bible has this unique quality. Other books may help, but it is in the Holy Scriptures that he breaks through and comes to you. The Holy Spirit lurks within its pages, and Jesus leaps from its pages to come into your heart.

Of course this most likely means that you want him to come. You read with a prayer that he will come. You may not understand everything at first, or ever. But if Jesus can walk out of the book into your life, then the most important thing has happened.

Another good reason for reading the Bible is to discover what God has done, is doing, and will do for you. Like a thread running through all 66 of its separate books, the Bible tells the story of God's love for you. He created you in love. He doesn't drop you when you do wrong, but keeps on loving you. And the great guarantee that he loves you is the wonderful story of Jesus, his Son, who came down from heaven to die for you so that all your sins can be forgiven and you live with God forever. And Jesus promised to be with you every day and night, until the end of life.

In all the religious books of the world, you will never find a story quite like that. The Bible keeps reminding and assuring you that, no matter what, God will never stop loving you. And you need to hear that over and over again.

Still another reason for reading it is that you will want to find out what Jesus wants you to do. Of course, you won't find a neat set of rules to cover every situation in life. You'll have to dig around a bit. Even then, you may be puzzled. But keep reading. Somehow God will help you find the way. The great truth that will keep coming to you is that you must love other people as the Lord has loved you. If you can set out to make your decisions according to this general rule, you will not go far wrong.

Remember, the Bible is not an encyclopedia. If you are to write an essay on dogs or stars, you would not first go to the Bible for information. God has other ways of letting us know about dogs and stars. But if you are to know about God's love, about how God deals with you and what he has promised for you in this life and the next, then you must go to the Bible.

Some people may tell you that the Bible is not reliable, that it is full of mistakes. But these are people who probably are looking for the wrong things in the Bible. They are not looking for God; in fact, they perhaps are looking for mistakes. They may tell you that the Bible has no idea how vast the universe is, nor does it contain adequate history. For God's purposes, this may not be important. After all, he is out to find you! And he will find you, if you go earnestly in search of him.

In any book of fiction, for instance, there is a climax. Everything builds up to a high point. This is true of the Bible too. Everything leads up to the coming of Jesus Christ. Even in the first chapters of Genesis there is a hint of his coming. And the very last of the books, Revelation, tells of his coming again.

If you have not bothered much with reading the Bible, the best way to start is to read one or more of the Gospels. Don't start with Genesis and read book after book in succession. Start with the Gospel of Mark, for instance. Get a good, readable modern translation. Read it in one sitting from beginning to end. It will take you an hour, at the most an hour and a half. Pretend that you have not met this Jesus before. Try to think that he is talking to you, and that he is at your very elbow, or sitting across from you in the room.

After reading all four of the Gospels, go on to some of the letters of the Apostle Paul—Philippians, for instance. Paul was the first great missionary who started one congregation after another in the Mediterranean world. Get the feel of what he and the other disciples thought of Jesus and how they witnessed to him.

Don't overlook some of the great books and chapters of the Old Testament. You will find some of the Psalms of great help, and some of the wonderful chapters in Isaiah. If you like poetry at all, the language of the Old Testament will get under your skin.

It may be of help to find some person who has read the Bible a long time, your pastor or someone else, and ask him what parts of the Bible have meant the most to him. He may even mark your Bible for you.

When you discover favorite passages, why not

memorize them? If you do, you will need to repeat them over and over, so that finally your tongue will take over, and these passages can come to your mind again and again wherever you are. They will become a source of comfort and courage for you.

It may help too if you adopt some kind of schedule of regular reading. It is easy to forget, day after day. But if you resolve that no day shall go by without some reading of the Good Book, you will be surprised to find yourself drawn step by step into its riches.

Give the Bible a chance. It is like a ship that carries God to you. You need not worship the book, but you will cherish it. You worship God and him alone, after all. But down through hundreds of years this book has been loved by millions as God's Word, and you will learn to love it too.

In a very profound sense, you do *not* find God there. God finds *you* there. He is in pursuit of you. He has been from the time you were born. And while God is not limited to a book, nonetheless he has chosen in a very singular way to reveal himself and to come to you through this great book.

Five

Hints

About Prayer

Old people sometimes talk to themselves. Perhaps you've listened to your grandmother. Working in the kitchen or wandering around looking for her glasses, she keeps up a conversation—with herself. It's a delightful habit.

Prayer is something different. It is not talking to yourself. It is talking to God. And God is not some fantasy. God is real.

A great many things can be said about prayer. I want to point you to five.

First, *you dial direct—anytime.* You need not call the operator and ask her to connect you with God. You have a direct line, and the line is open 24 hours a day the whole year through.

This is as wonderful as it is strange. You have never seen God, and you will not hear his voice on the other end. He is busy managing this vast universe. He also has about three billion other direct lines from earth. Every living person in the world is given a direct line. Many never use it, but it is there anytime they think to dial. How it is possible for God to give such personal attention to so many lines is a mystery. But then God is God, and there is no limit to what he can do.

You may have fixed times for prayer, when you sit down to eat, or when you go to bed, and of course when you go to church. But the line is always open. You may pray when you write a test or when you enter a race. You may pray when suddenly you face some sort of danger. God never stops listening. It is wise to have fixed times, because otherwise you may forget to call on him altogether. And this would be tragic, because through prayer he has so much to give you.

Second, *you reach love when you pray.* God is the heart of love. He is in fact the source of love. He loves you more than any human being can ever love you. He wants to swallow you up in love, so that you rest back into his arms of love and, in turn, find it possible to spread love throughout the world.

Prayer would be worthwhile even if it were no more than asking your school principal for a favor or some employer for a job. But the wonderful thing about God is that you are in touch with the very center of all love. He can give you a favor or a job, but whatever he gives he gives in love.

His love is best known through what Jesus Christ has done for us, and still continues to do. Jesus died on a cross for us. In him we have forgiveness for all our sins. In him we have the guarantee that God receives us as his children no matter how often we forget him or fail him—

if we do not turn away from him. If you ever doubt that God loves you, remember that he sent his only Son to die for us. What greater assurance can there be?

If you have had a falling out with some friend, with Jane for instance, you may not feel very easy about calling her. Will she even talk to you? Will she forgive you? Perhaps she is too hurt to forget and be your friend again. God is not Jane. God loves with an everlasting love. If you have wronged him, he is hurt, to be sure. But God does not sulk. He never holds a grudge. He waits more eagerly than ever for your call. He is always your friend.

Third, *you get answers*. You cannot hear him. You may never quite know how he answers. If you ask for a specific thing, like a job, you may not get it. And why? Perhaps God has something better in mind for you. After all, he knows much better than you what is best for you. Sometimes he delays. He may know that you are not yet ready to receive what you ask. You will need to trust him. Only be sure that he loves you, that he hears you, and that he is at work to give you blessings beyond your wildest imagination.

Remember, too, that both you and other people may block him from doing what you want. He has given you the power to do foolish and wicked things, and he has given this power to all people. By our ignorance and wickedness we may prevent his plans for us. In a war, for instance, millions of people pray for the war to end, but the war rolls on—because in our stupidity and greed we keep the war going. Or, even in as simple a prayer as "God, let me pass this course," you may fail to do your share of studying, and you fail the course—not because God failed to answer your prayer, but because you failed him.

God wants only what is good for us. Tragedy, sin, pain, and death have come to this world, not because God willed them, but in spite of God. He did not want cancer and accidents and war to kill his children. And when these things happen, he is near us to give us strength and comfort to endure them.

Fourth, *you flirt with danger when you pray.* In as simple a prayer as the Lord's Prayer, think of what you are asking: thy kingdom come; thy will be done on earth as in heaven. Have we ever really thought what changes would come in our lives if in every single instance his will—and not ours—were to govern? Would we really like that? And suppose the ways of his kingdom were to replace our style of life, would we like that?

Praying to God is to risk being captured by God. It is not like telephoning the department store and asking that they send out a dress or a suit on the next delivery. You need never know the clerk at the other end of the wire. After all, you are interested only in getting the dress or the suit. But suppose that you got the clerk too, and that he settled down in your house and never left, and that he insisted on having you do what he wanted to do.

God is not interested alone in giving you the things you need for this life, like food and clothing and friends. He is interested in giving you himself. In a strange and wonderful way he comes to live in and with us. We become both his house and his follower. He lives in us and he lures us into following him.

And think where this might lead us. Coming to Jesus may seem like a good thing, but if we come to him, or he to us, then we are trapped into going where he goes. We will need to take a hard look at where he is likely to go, and where he is likely to lead us. We will find ourselves involved in every person in need. We will be led into fights for justice and mercy for all men. We may have to suffer. After all, he suffered, even a cross. These are the risks we take.

Fifth, *you will touch a new world when you pray*. And it is a glorious world. God presides over this "invisible" kingdom, as he also presides over everything. We may miss the glories of the invisible kingdom, if we don't pray. If we do pray, and pray in earnest, we will be walking into a vast and wonderful world that opens only to the eyes and ears of faith.

There are people who turn from this invisible kingdom as if it were some fairy tale, some fantasy, open only to children and simple-minded people. They think that intelligent people will go by the proofs of the laboratory and nothing more. The fact is that throughout the centuries some of the most intelligent people in the world have been disciples of Jesus, have known the riches of prayer, and have lived in the mystery and the wonder of the kingdom of God.

Here in this kingdom are the fountains of love, of joy, of peace, of patience, of courage, and of hope. How foolish of us not to open our lives to these priceless gifts. How wise we are to open the doors. How wise we are to pray!

Why
Have a Job
At All?

People will ask you, "What are you going to be (or do) when you finish school? Doctor? Taxi-driver? Nurse? Farmer? Preacher? Salesman? Artist? Teacher?"

Why do anything at all?

Suppose there are enough teachers and nurses and farmers. Suppose there are already more people than necessary for almost every job. No one is crying for anyone. Why not drop out of the job market altogether? Let the people work who want to work, and you get out of the way.

Why not? Of course your folks wouldn't like it. They want you to make something of yourself, to be successful at something. And maybe that's a good enough reason to get prepared to have a respectable job. But maybe not. There ought to be some other reasons. You can drift around for a few years, but what will you do when you're 40 or 50? To drift your whole life through may not be a happy prospect.

Let's think of a few reasons for getting set for some particular job. The first and most obvious reason is that we can't have everyone copping out. Then there'd be no doctors or farmers or preachers or plumbers. The world must have them, simply to keep life going. But you might ask, "Why me?" But why not you? Why should you drop out of the game and let someone else carry on?

Or, you might be asking why this kind of world should keep going. We have wars. We have pollution. We have people spurning each other simply because their skins are of different color. Why should you become an engineer and help the world discover new weapons? Why should you become a doctor and help people live to be 150 years old when they don't want to live that long? Why should you be a salesman and press people to buy three times as many things as they need? Why should you work hard to become rich when others will become poor?

If you turn this kind of world down—give it up as an undesirable world—do you help the situation by sitting by some lake or by hitchhiking across the country? If you don't like this kind of world, what kind do you want? And how do you get it? Not by running off. In fact, you may have to become a doctor or an engineer or a statesman or a preacher or a farmer to be in a position to do something about it.

We get ourselves maneuvered into a corner. To cop out is to let the world go to the dogs, if that's where it's going. To do something about it is to get a job, get into the stream, find a vantage point of influence, and do battle for a better world.

All right! You plan for a job, or vocation. Now, what kind? How do you find your place in this world of work?

One of the common notions of our time is that a person should choose a job in which he has some natural aptitudes or skills and which he likes to do. These are the two guidelines: aptitude and desire. If you have an aptitude for mathematics and like mathematics, by this rule you should be an engineer or scientist. If you have an aptitude for speech and communication and you like to give speeches, by this rule you should probably be a preacher or an auctioneer.

Helpful as these guidelines are, they are basically wrong. Suppose you have skills in breaking locks and you like to rob banks; this does not mean you have a calling to rob banks. If you do something well and you like to do it, it still may be utterly wrong to do it. Much of the vocational guidance given in school follows this line. But it is not good enough, as you can easily see.

I knew a young man who had straight A's through college in physics and mathematics. He came to a theological seminary to become a pastor. Why, I asked him? His answer was quite simple, "Because I think God wants me to preach the gospel and help people through the church." Of course he could still have done this as an engineer or scientist. But the point is that he was guided by something more than aptitudes. He may have been a better scientist than he will be a pastor, who knows. But for him a job was more than doing what he could do well or what he might like to do. He had asked himself, "What *ought* I do?" or, "What does God want me to do?"

I knew another young man who had planned from childhood to be a preacher. When he was ready to come to the seminary, he wrote me that he believed the Lord was directing him to politics and government. He discovered that he had a natural talent for leadership, and he was convinced that "the storm centers" for making the world better for his own country and for the world lay in the area of government. He hoped some day to be a senator and to give himself to the causes of peace and justice. He believed that the Lord was directing him, and this was what he had to do.

What the Lord is most concerned about for you is that you be his follower, his disciple, no matter what occupation you may have. He needs followers in all jobs—law, science, business, medicine, education. He needs people everywhere who will decide what to do—not by what he likes to do or by what he does well—but by asking, "What would my Lord want me to do?"

The world really needs you. It does not need you merely to drift through life, finding something interesting to do now and then. It needs you to make a better world. You may not succeed. You are only one, after all. But you are one. And the capacities you have, whatever they are, should be invested in making a better world.

And there are all sorts of wonderful opportunities for anyone who is serious about putting his abilities to use. There may be unemployment in some occupations now and then. But the world can always use a person who prepares himself with skills and who will give unstintingly of his energies. The Lord may have some specific occupation cut out for you, but this is only a secondary concern for him. Whatever necessary or honorable occupation you choose, he can use you richly there as his follower.

Every follower of the Lord has the same vocation, no matter what his job. Each of us who sets out to follow Jesus must be concerned with other people. We are to love them, as he has loved us. This is the overarching command—and job.

You've already got a job; in fact, many jobs. If you are a student you have an assignment from God: to do your studies well, to respect your teachers, to be a friend to every other student. You are a son or daughter in a home; that's another job. Your parents, often worried about many things, need your encouragement and cheer. The task of being a disciple or follower of Jesus, in school and at home, is after all a major job. Long before you get a paycheck, you are already employed.

Years ago we had few machines. Most of the work had to be done by hand. Most jobs were at least six days a week, and often ten hours a day. Now, with all sorts of mechanical slaves, we end up with more leisure time in most regular occupations.

This leisure opens up all sorts of interesting ideas for additional "jobs." People have time to seek out other people who are in need, people who

need encouragement, people who are really waiting for someone to be their friend. You will get
no salary for this. But these are jobs, nonetheless,
and in the Lord's sight they may be more important than the job which earns you a living.

Why work at all? There are a hundred reasons.
Most of all, we work because we are on God's
payroll to make the world a better place.

When

I

Marry

Marriage is not the most important thing in life, but very nearly so. A good and happy marriage can be the channel for hundreds of blessings. A miserable or broken marriage becomes one of life's heaviest burdens.

Before you stand at the altar and promise God to love, cherish and honor each other for a lifetime, come what may, you should have spent a lot of time thinking what this will mean for you. Marriage is not a come-and-go affair.

It is true that many marriages flounder on the rocks and end in divorce. But divorce is always unhappy. If not a tragedy, it is always sadness. No one can escape being hurt. And in almost every instance if more thought had been given before the wedding and more patience and love had been used after the wedding, the marriage could have been saved.

You will have all sorts of friends during a lifetime, but you will have (or at least should have normally) one wife or one husband. You had better choose with care.

First, you must ask what you will bring to the marriage. Are you the kind of person who is selfish, critical, stubborn? Is it your habit to choose friends primarily because of what these friends can do for you? Are you hung up on finding *your* identity, doing *your* "thing," developing *your* personality? When you fail, do you pin the blame on others—your parents, your teachers, your associates? Does your life center on yourself, so that people and things are good if they serve *you?*

If you are this kind of person, you probably should not marry at all. It is one thing to use friends for your selfish interests; it is catastrophic if you use your wife or husband for yourself. Marriage is not even a 50-50 enterprise, each going half way or contributing to a fair share. A good marriage means that each one sets out to serve the other, if need be going the whole distance and not only half way. Until each is primarily concerned about the care of or happiness of the other, the marriage will fail to have the enchantment and strength that it should have. You do not *use* each other; you give yourselves to each other.

Another thing to remember is that while marriage is principally a matter between two people alone, the two of you really are not alone. Each of you comes from a family, belongs to a church most likely, has convictions and tastes in many things. How much alike should you be? Should you come from the same kind of families, the same race, the same religion? Perhaps, but not necessarily. Many marriages have crossed cultural and religious lines, even racial and national, and have been good durable marriages. Two people who love each other dearly can overcome many differences.

But remember that you do bring to your marriage everything you are, and what you are is determined in much measure by your background —where you belong. It takes strong people who love each other very much to come from vastly different backgrounds.

It is a wonderful thing if your families and friends and community can say, "Isn't it grand that these two people chose each other!" Approval of those to whom you already belong is a strengthening thing for any marriage. Even so, the success of the marriage will be up to you.

Among the many things you each bring to your marriage, your sex life will be one of the most important and the most mysterious. Sexual needs are not like the need for food or water. You can eat and drink alone. The need each has for sexual expression, while indeed a need, involves two people. It is the most profound way of communicating between two people. You may give yourselves to each other through kind words and generous deeds. But it is in the sexual act that you give yourselves to each other most deeply. It is for that reason that sex should be saved for the one person who will share your life most profoundly for a lifetime.

Remember, too, that you must be ready to live with each other as you are, not as you hope to be. Jane was sure she loved Bob, but she did not like his profanity or his careless use of alcohol. She married him, thinking that their love and life together would change things. She was terribly mistaken, and their marriage was unhappy in many ways because Bob did not change.

Each person who marries should be sure that he or she finds much to enjoy in the other person and should set out not to change anyone, but each to enjoy the other throughout the years. Most likely each will change in a quiet way, but never because one or the other has been in a campaign to accomplish change. You don't marry to reform someone.

Religion is a matter in which the two should either have very much in common or should be able to respect deeply their differences. You can stand to have someone laugh at your politics, disagree with your taste in music, fail to share your desire for sports, but it's far more difficult if the person you marry does not share your faith or even makes fun of it or opposes it.

Again, if you can come to each other with the same faith, a primary commitment to the Lord, and can share worship and prayer together, you have a basis for meeting your sorrows, anxieties, fears, hostilities which nothing else can provide. If you know what it is to be forgiven by Christ, you can turn to each other to be forgiving and to be forgiven. Even devout Christians will have their trials and troubles in marriage, but they know where to go for inner strength.

Many people, when they are young, tend to think religion may not be important, but they discover as the years go on that if they can share a faith together, go to church together, bring up their children in the same faith, they have something that ties them together in a wonderful way.

To succeed in making a good home, where husband and wife truly love one another and where the children feel the security of their love, is perhaps the greatest single achievement in life—greater than being elected president of the United States or being a star on television.

If you become a wife and mother and someone asks you what you do, under no circumstances should you reply, "I'm only a homemaker." *Only* a homemaker? You might as well say, if you are a career woman, "I'm only an architect—or only a bank president—or only a doctor." There is no career as exalted or exacting as creating a home in which love and faith and courage are woven into the lives of parents and children. This is really the laboratory, the workshop, for almost everything good that may come to the world.

As a husband and father, you will know this too. Your business or profession is your second occupation. The first is your home. Fail there, and whatever success you may have in the affairs of the world will seem incomplete. Most men feel this way. A business man may have on his office desk a picture of his wife and three children. If one day he gets a phone call saying that all had been killed in an accident, suddenly he wonders why he should keep on in business at all. It was for them that he struggled to do things well in the world of business.

All of us, parents and children, will need daily forgiveness from each other. None of us will measure up. Mothers and fathers are often harried and worried and overlook the needs of their children. Children, not understanding the strains the world puts on their parents, may have a hard time being charitable and forgiving.

A good home is the center of civilization. It is a goal worth giving the most careful preparation to achieve. When and if you marry, you will undertake the most glorious and the most exacting job in life.

Do You Feel Sorry for Parents?

Perhaps you should feel sorry for them. After all, they have you on their hands! Of course, they chose to have you; you didn't ask to have them. Parents are never perfect, and neither are children. How children and parents get along is never perfect either, therefore.

I like the Bible because it is frank about how parents and children often failed each other. It's a realistic book. Jacob treated two of his sons better than the other ten; Absalom rebelled against his father David. No one is pictured as perfect in the Bible except Jesus himself.

If we are going to talk about parents at all, the very first thing we must know is that none of them are as good as they ought to be. And that goes for the best of them.

Almost every book you read has something about parents failing their children. Do we ever read anything about how the children may be forgetting about their parents? Hardly ever.

Let's spend a few minutes feeling sorry for parents, shall we?

It's not easy to be young these days. Perhaps it has never been. But today we hear all sorts of things about an uncertain future for our country and for the world. Maybe someone will trigger an atomic blast. Maybe the planet will be overrun by an exploding population. Maybe the computer will replace people and there'll be no jobs. If you want to find things to worry about, you don't have to look far or read much.

How about the worries of parents? Maybe they're more worried than you are. If they are responsible parents at all—and most of them are —they may be more worried for you than you are for yourself. They want the very best for you. In fact, most of them want a better life for you than they ask for themselves. They not only worry for themselves; they worry even more for you. It's only fair, therefore, that you start worrying for them a little too.

When I was a boy of 12 my father took me to a distant city on a buying trip. We took an overnight train, and for the first time I slept in a pullman berth. I remember the porter patting my head and asking, "Are you going to be as good a man as your father?" to which my father gave quick reply, "He's going to be a much better man." I think he was expressing a universal hope of all fathers. Fifty years later, I am still trying to be as good a man as my father.

Modern life has put new strains on the home. Most people live in cities. Perhaps both father and mother have jobs, and come home at different hours. Children also scatter to and from varied activities. It was not so a couple generations ago when most people probably lived on farms. Everyone in the family worked together, played together, and worshipped together. Divorce was virtually unknown.

Today many children are faced with parents who have separated and no longer live together. A divorce makes it even more difficult for children to feel sorry for their parents. They are likely to accuse them of not having enough love or strength of character to keep the home together, and fight a bitterness. It takes a great deal of charity and maturity to feel sorry for parents who have failed to keep their home together. Most likely they still love their children very much. It is wonderful if the children can be understanding and forgiving.

Most parents are much more proud of their children than the children will ever know. They will boast of their sons' and daughters' achievement to others when they may neglect to say much to their children.

And many a father and mother hide their worries from their children. Why should they dump a load on their young shoulders? Many a young person has had to grow up to become a parent himself before he realized what secret fears and anxieties his parents may have been carrying for him.

It is most natural for you to want your parents to trust you. Most of them do most of the time. But in their concern for you, they may seem not to trust you. Why don't they go to bed and to sleep when the night hours tick away and you're not yet at home? Before you become angry, remember that fifty thousand people are killed on the highways each year, and the majority are young people. One of the names in the morning paper could be your name. Wouldn't you really be disappointed if they did not have some fears, even if these fears seem to indicate that they don't trust you?

I am a parent, and now a grandparent. I'll let you in on a few secrets. No parent every really stops worrying. Even when you are grown and away from home, they still have you in the center. And they will start all over again when you have children, their grandchildren. And I am sure that it is true of most parents that when they list the things they thank God for, you are at the top of the list. They pray, "Thank you, God, for Mary, and bless her; thank you, God, for Bill, and bless him."

They can't let you go. Their love for you is something like God's love. You can't stop God from loving you. If you turn from him, forget all about him, disobey him and even curse him, God still keeps on loving you. While parents are known at long last to give up on a son or daughter—and this is rare—even then there is an empty place ready to be filled with love. I knew a man who as a youth ran away from home and was not heard of for six years. He never wrote a note; it was as if he had simply dropped out of the world. One Christmas he came home. Love was waiting for him as if he had never been gone.

There is a familiar story about a young man who had left home, had fallen into evil ways, had spent a term in prison and had never answered any of his folks' letters. One day they got a short letter, "I'm coming home. But can you ever forgive me? I'll be on the 3:30 train. If you forgive me, tie a white ribbon on a branch of the old elm tree at the edge of town, and I'll get off at the station. If not, I'll go right through." As the train rounded the bend and the tree came into view he caught sight of white ribbons floating from every branch of the tree. A parent's love is often like that.

It's not easy to be 30 or 40 or 50 years old these days either. A father will ask himself, "What will happen to my children if I lose my job, if my health fails, if I die?" And even more than that, "What if my boy or girl gives up, is fed up with school, turns to drugs or alcohol, runs around with a cruel and calloused crowd?"

There is no one who can cheer up a discouraged parent as you can. The praise of the world around them is nothing compared with your praise. A kind word from you is worth a thousand from others. Fathers' Day and Mothers' Day may be occasions for a gift or a corsage of flowers, but you can forget these days altogether if day after day you remember to show some kindness and understanding.

Words are not that all important, but they are still wonderful. "Kind words can never die; God alone knows how deep they lie, hidden in the breast." A genuine word of thanks from you will never be forgotten.

Most important to any parent, of course, is the style of life that you live. The world may not call you a success, but if you live the kind of life that allows your parents to be proud of you, nothing can compare with that.

God will have to forgive all of us, fathers and mothers and sons and daughters, for our having failed each other in many ways. Fortunately, there is such a forgiveness with God. But it is wonderful if we can give each other the kind of memories that we can treasure as the years go on.

The Good Old Days

Your grandfather may tell you about the good old days when he was a young man. He may even go farther back into history, way back hundreds of years, and imply that today is bad, very bad, and that you have a very bleak future.

Fine a man as your grandfather may be, he probably is no expert historian, nor does he sort out his own memories very well.

If he worked on a farm as a young man, these "good old days" meant that he got up at 5 A.M. and worked till dark, without running water, without electricity, without telephone and without seeing many friends.

These old days were not altogether good, not by the widest stretch of the imagination. People died from all sorts of diseases which medicine has now overcome. And there was violence then too.

Or go a bit farther back into history. Why do you think Europe, for instance, is punctuated by ancient forts? This was the only way for one group or tribe or nation to keep from being annihilated or captured by marauding enemies.

101

The world has never been a period of "the good old days." We have always had the problems that come from greed, fear and selfishness. Today is no different.

Only this. We have far greater resources to deal with these problems today. We have machines to replace the drudgery of millions of people. We have transportation to bring help to millions. We have medical science to postpone the march of death for millions. A scientist friend of mine told me that we are within reach of new sources of power with which we can convert all the salt water we want into fresh water and pump it through conduits to any part of the world. The Sahara desert can bloom like the rose and all the arid regions of Asia can be gardens.

It is true that we can use this power to destroy one another. The future is more threatening on the one hand, and infinitely more promising on the other hand. It is a glorious day to be alive and young, also frightening.

If you want to look at the dark side, go ahead. You can bemoan the pollution of air and water, you can deplore the growing population of the earth, you can have nightmares over the bomb. And when the picture is dark enough, you can retreat to drugs or alcohol or just drift around. You simply cop out, without being bold enough to commit suicide.

Even if the world were to blow up tomorrow, it would be a pity to spend your last days in drugs or alcohol or just standing around. Besides, it's

102

probably not going to blow up tomorrow, or next year, or ever. It's God's earth, and he will not let it get out of hand. He may have unpredictable plans and blessings in store for it, and he wants you involved in bringing them to be.

Looked at from any historic perspective, the twentieth century cannot possibly be the worst of all possible centuries. In spite of two World Wars, a Korean war and the perplexing and unhappy Vietnam war, in no other century has so much sheer drudgery been overcome, so much poverty conquered, so much hunger and disease pushed back, so many non-white people awakened to greater justice and so much education made available to so many. There are massive tasks yet to do, but the young generation gives evidence of understanding both the risks and the opportunities.

Changes have come so fast that we are both exhilarated and frightened. But it may well be that in a period of change God has a better chance to lead us to significant achievements than in a period of calm and security.

As we face the future, there are a few simple yet profound truths to remember. The first is that God is around. He has not abandoned this planet. He loved it so much that he sent his only begotten son to die for it. He wants us as his children, now and forever. We disappoint him terribly. But he does not give us up. He forgives and forgives, and keeps helping us in every good task. He puts limits to our evil ways and strengthens our good ways. Some day our Lord will return to judge everything and everybody, but until then he will never for a moment forsake us.

A second thing to remember is that we cannot know when something may actually be good when we think it bad. A man missed his plane by five minutes, and this meant he would miss his son's wedding. Unhappy and angry, he returned to his hotel to telephone his home. He chanced to hear a radio flash about a plane crash. It was the one he would have taken had he not had the "bad luck" of missing departure. This illustration is perhaps too simple, but many things that we think to be unfortunate may in later outcome be understood as good. Only in the longer retrospect of history can we know what the events of today may produce.

Also, many of the blessings which the Lord assuredly wants us to have may require some painful preparation on our part. We believe in free government, for instance, and we believe that God too wants this kind of self-determination for all men. But it takes both wisdom and responsibility to govern, and some peoples that have never had any self-government may need years and years of painful grooming before they are ready. And we, too, who live in a democracy, must undergo the pain of effort and discipline if we are to keep the gift of political freedom. In every area of life we need to remember that God's great gifts to us may always entail some suffering.

Then, too, God does not hold us responsible for the long future; he gives us tasks for today. We live one day at a time, and we must give account for tasks and responsibilities here and now. Today is today, and tomorrow has not yet arrived. Many people, looking into the long future, are paralyzed by fears of what may come to such an extent that they overlook the many "little" things that the Lord expects of them today. They are robbed of the pleasures and the duties which might have made each day full and rich.

Suppose in reading a book about India you become so agitated over the woes of that country that you forget to be courteous to your friends, you overlook the people in the next block who need your help and you become moody and cheerless in your own home. Would you not have gotten your priorities all mixed up? There is nothing wrong about your concern for India and her future, but not at the expense of concerns near at hand. You may do little for India, you may do much for the people in the next block.

And what you do for the people in the next block may in God's great plan become a part of a larger whole. It may become a link in a long chain which profoundly affects the future.

Most of you will not be elected president of the United States or a U.S. Senator, or governor of a state. You may decide that your chances of influencing the future may be quite meager. But who knows what little things become big things in the fabric of history which God and man "weave together." Who made Abraham Lincoln the kind of man he was? His back-woods mother? Some kindness from a forgotten friend? Some incident way back in his childhood? Very often it is little things that shape people, and people shape history and the future.

Best of all, God is in the future, and we dare not sell him short.

Beyond
Death

The years are piling up for me. Death is not too far from the door. But who knows how far? He may be nearer your door than mine. We had a son die at twenty-four, and a nephew at fifteen.

From the time we are old enough to wonder about things, we have thought about death. It is the one certain thing that will happen to each of us. Death ties us together and makes us one family.

In the early days of our land the immigrants faced death around every corner. There were few doctors, and they did not yet have many of today's medicines. Thousands died from smallpox, diphtheria, measles, pneumonia; now hardly anyone dies from these. But people still die.

There are times when a person may want to die. Fears and disappointments may crowd in until you see no way out but death. Psychologists tell us that "the death-wish" is not uncommon for most of us at some time or another. Fortunately it is not strong enough for us to do anything about it. Suicides after all are not common.

The "life-wish" is stronger. I don't want to die. I love the scudding clouds, the warm greeting of my friend, the excitement of a football game. God has given us life to use and to enjoy. It would be a pity if I allowed some fears and failures to rob me of the many wonderful things that the years can bring.

Many years ago I knew a girl who tried to end it. She swallowed a bottle of sleeping pills. Fortunately some friends found her and rushed her to the hospital. Now, years later, married to a doctor and with a fine family of her own, she must look back upon that moment of fear and despair with regret, and with great thanks that help came before it was too late.

Every person has periods of deep disappointments. Things look dark. You may say, "I wish I had never been born." But there are all sorts of bright spots, if we will but look for them. Death is never the answer.

Death is not a friend. It may appear so to a man whose body is wasting away by cancer and there is no hope of recovery. He may pray for death to come soon. But death itself, which began its march with the first signs of cancer, is not the friend. Life is the friend. God gave life. Death came in through the back door. The Bible itself calls death "the last enemy."

When death comes, God uses it as a doorway to usher us into a new and greater life. But the Lord is not on the side of death; he is always on the side of life. He does not put us on a journey from life to death; his ticket reads "from death to life." On an Easter morning he overcame death, and he intends that we shall overcome it too. Because he lives, we too shall live when death is done with us and can do no more. There is a resurrection to eternal life for all who rest in Jesus.

It is important not to blame God for death. My son at twenty-four was killed instantly in a street accident. My nephew at fifteen died of a brain tumor. It was not God who engineered the accident or sent the tumor. God wanted life for these young men, and did not want them so soon transferred to heaven.

I might very well ask, "If God did not want it, and if God is all-powerful, why did he allow death to come?" I have no answer. I only know that the Bible is quite clear in not having God responsible for all the deaths, and that he has set in motion a great plan to have death altogether gone. Why he does not finish this job at once and have tragedy and sin and pain and death forever gone, I do not know. He will in his own good time.

In the meantime, we are to accept life as the opportunity for all sorts of good. No matter if we have dark days of fear and frustration and wonder if it's all worth keeping on, we are to remember that God is on the side of life and that Jesus came to earth to lead us through all sorts of open doors. You can't possibly know all the great things he has in store for you, if you will let him take over.

Death will come of course. But we are not to

hurry it along, nor hope for it to come. When it comes, it has victory only for an instant. God has a life for us beyond death.

Even if life were no more than the years between birth and death, I suppose we should thank God for those short years, mixed as they are with pain and pleasure, failure and success. If fifteen years, fine; if twenty-four, good; if seventy, O.K.

But God promises more, much more. There is life on the other side of death. This life is not a mere extension of the kind we have here. On the other side, all the shortcomings and pains on this side will be gone.

Before Jesus left this earth he told his followers, "Let not your hearts be troubled; believe in God, believe also in me. In my Father's house are many rooms; if it were not so, would I have told you that I go to prepare a place for you? And when I go and prepare a place for you, I will come again and will take you to myself, that where I am you may be also."

I asked a young man of 17 if he had given much thought to heaven and he answered, "No, not really. I am more concerned about what this earth will be like. It is enough for me to know that when I die I will be with the Lord."

We may not spend much time wondering what heaven will be like, but one thing is sure: God must have wonderful things waiting for us on the other side. We can let our imaginations run almost riot in trying to think of them. "What no eye has seen, nor ear heard, nor the heart of man conceived, what God has prepared for them who love him." Throughout the Bible God tantalizes us and enraptures us with the love that will swallow us up when death is through.

Is it not exciting to think of the great company of people already living in that wonderful sector of God's empire? In the book of Hebrews the Lord pictures those who have died as sitting in some vast bleacher section, cheering us on. We are still on earth, running the race. Their race is over. They have won and are now the spectators. How much they share the life that we live, we cannot know. But dare we set limits on God? Perhaps there is more contact from the other side than we think.

Perhaps we should be willing to settle for the Lord's blessings on this side of death and not be greedy to have even more on the other side. After all, God is lavish with his gifts on this side. Why ask for more?

Let us say that God is greedy. He does not want you only for a few swift years here on earth. He wants you in heaven with him forevermore. This is his way of saying that you count. You count for much more than you can ever know.

Many of us have trouble thinking that we really count. The world does not seem to need us. Our friends may come and go; they don't seem to need us. But God says "I need you. I want you for myself, not only now. I want you in my great kingdom to live with me always." Even if you fail him again and again, and must come to him to be forgiven a thousand times, even then he wants you. Can you think of anything that makes you as important as that does?

Life beyond death is God's way of saying that he loves you, not for a day, not only when you are good or successful, but that he loves you so much that he never wants it to end for you and for him.